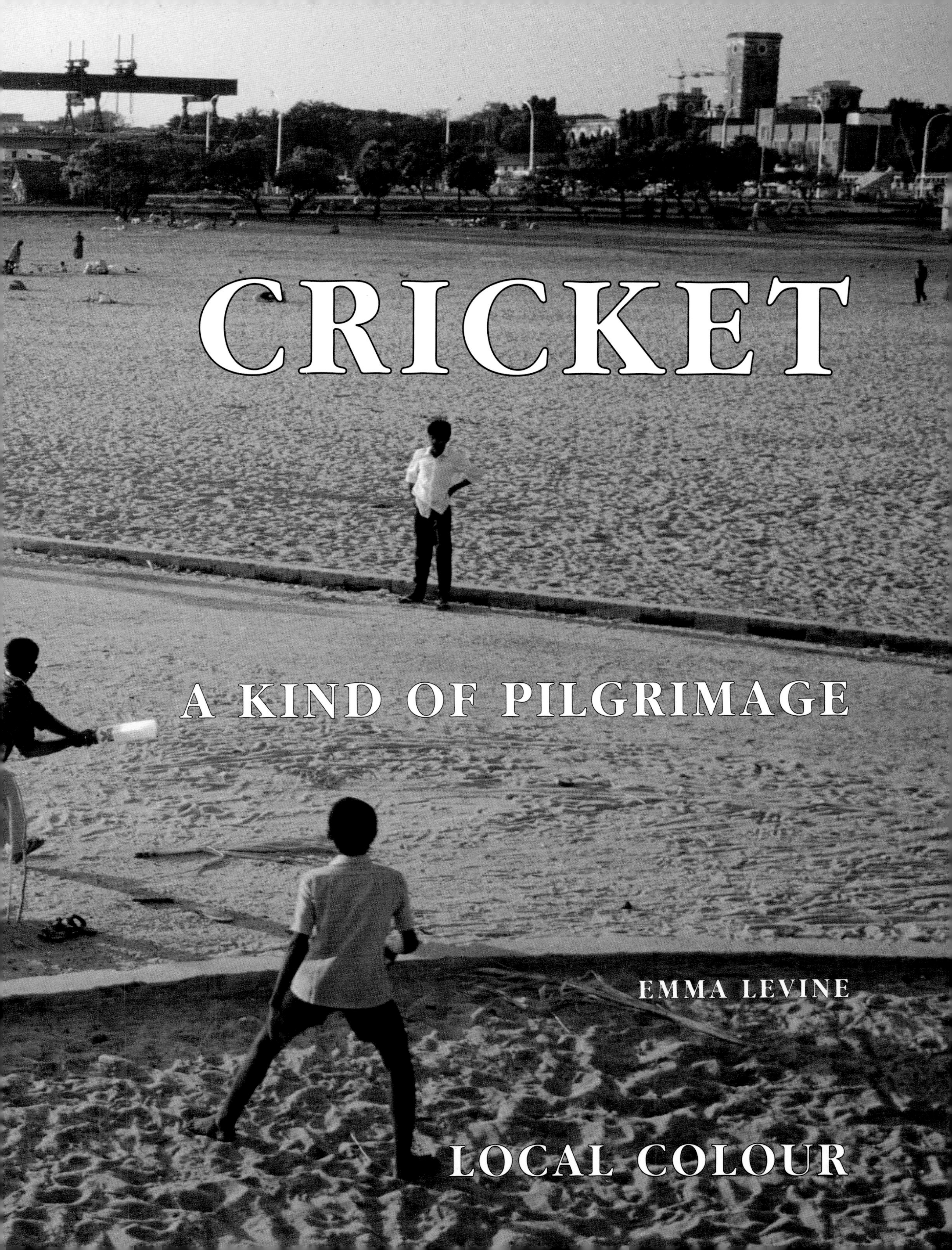

CRICKET

A KIND OF PILGRIMAGE

EMMA LEVINE

LOCAL COLOUR

Designed by Richard Hasslam

ISBN 962-217-453-1

Printed in Hong Kong

CONTENTS

To Mum, Dad, Iain, Simon (who taught me how to bowl straight) and Colin.

ACKNOWLEDGEMENTS

The trip would not have been possible—or as enjoyable—without the help and hospitality of many people, and in particular my thanks to:

Dom and Leela Moreas, Hemant Kenkre, Gulu Ezekiel, Dr. Sareen, Mr. Vasisht, Mr. Thaker, V.J. Vijendra Rao, Sanjay Singh, Tahil Menon, Jamil Sakrani, Imtiaz Sipra, Sikander Bakht, Sarfaraz Nawaz, Salahuddin Haider, Amjad Aziz Malik, Nigel Cullum, Tilak de Zoysa, Tarik Raz, Puneet Anand, Terence Mudalige, Prakash Bhandari, Sabya Sachi Sarker, Gul Hameed Bhatti, Abdul Rasheed Shakoor, Tariq Ansari, Hanif Mohammad, Dr. Mohammad Ali Shah, Ashraf Ali, Mr. Zaidi, Ashiq Qureshi, Khawir Khawaja, Peter Slack, Stephen Findley, William McLanachan and Peter Simpson .

Thanks must also go to my friends in Hong Kong for their strong support throughout this project, and especially to Stuart and Anne Hellier, whose patience and wonderful kindness made this possible.

Finally, my thanks to all the cricket officials, players and journalists who were a constant source of valuable information.

The generous support of Kodak (India) is greatly appreciated, especially Yolanda Fernandez and Sudarshan Bannerjee, for supplying all the films.

PREFACE

Cricket must surely be one of the strangest games ever to be invented by man and an even stranger relic of the British Raj in South Asia. Even in England where the game of cricket was born, let alone most of the world, many people cannot understand how, after five long days in a Test match, a game will often end without a result.

It is only in South Asia that a piece of willow and a small red ball are worshipped with such intensity. Cricket can unite and sometimes disunite the subcontinent.

One has to experience the Galle Face Green in Colombo on a Sunday morning teeming with games, so many that it is almost as crowded as Blackpool beach in the middle of summer; or the noise of over one hundred thousand fanatical supporters at Calcutta's Eden Gardens; or a game being played at 2,444 metres in the foothills of the Himalaya, almost twice the height of Ben Nevis.

This book is a celebration of cricket wherever it is played throughout South Asia: in the back alleys of Old Delhi only eight feet wide, where to attempt a square cut or a hook would be suicidal; or in the searing heat of a Rajasthani desert; at the venerable Calcutta Cricket and Football Club (only the hallowed MCC is older) or the night box-cricket game that was being played in Lahore under floodlights long before Kerry Packer invented his modern pyjama game.

This unique book captures the complete spectrum of cricket as it is played in South Asia, where unbridled passion will be building up as we approach the next Cricket World Cup.

Cricket—a religion or a sport?

Mark Tully

CRICKET MANIA

The sound of firecrackers and joyous, dancing feet pounding the streets of Old Delhi behind the bazaars of Chandni Chowk, suddenly began filling my ears in the stone courtyard I temporarily called home. This excessive noise puzzled me—but then this was my first trip to India, after all; I had only been in town for four days and customs and cultures were still being discovered. "Is it a wedding party?" I enquired from my hosts, referring to the commotion that was uniting singing paan-sellers, rickshaw wallahs, bank clerks and police officers together in exuberant celebrations on the streets.

They looked at me with a combination of hilarity and shock. Taking my arm, the father of the house, rocking with laughter, explained: "They are celebrating because India won the cricket match," he said delightedly. Celebrating a cricket match? Well, it was more than a cricket match. The 1992 World Cup match between arch rivals India and Pakistan, beamed live from Australia into almost every living room in the locality, had just finished and the party had just started.

Until that moment, I had lived in the comfortable ignorance that cricket was merely a sport taught by the British to the natives wherever they landed. Here, I thought, surely leather-on-willow could only be a "hangover" from colonial days. But these wild celebrations opened my eyes to a different world. For it dawned on me that I was now in a land where cricket was not just a sport played on lazy Sundays on village greens where cucumber sandwiches are washed down with tea or real ale. Here it was a vibrant culture; an obsession, a national identity and most importantly, a way of life. I was also to discover that Pakistan and Sri Lanka share a similar passion for the game but both countries display their own unique characteristics.

As soon as I discovered the answer to the noisy street celebrations in Old Delhi, my journey had begun; a kind of pilgrimage to the cricketing subcontinent. So, with a love for the game that must surely run deep through my Yorkshire blood, I began to stalk the subcontinent's cricketers and grounds, visiting a vast number of destinations and embarking on a series of unforgettable adventures spanning three countries.

In the backstreets of Calcutta I discovered shoeless boys playing and dreaming of being the next Sachin Tendulkar. I observed the tennis-ball night tournaments in Lahore with 265 dedicated teams participating; the annual college Big Matches in Colombo which highlights the sporting year as well as being the most prestigious occasion in the social calendar; the glorious maidans in Churchgate, the financial hub of Bombay where office clerks swap shirts, ties and briefcases for whites for two hours of daily practice before or after work; Afghan

(opposite) *A typical afternoon at the Azad Maidan, in Churchgate, Bombay. Side by side wickets mark the distinctive concept of maidan cricket.*

refugees in Pakistan's Northern Frontier who play in the high-walled enclosures of their homes between washing lines; schoolboys wiping sleep from their eyes stumbling to coaching sessions every Sunday at 6 am as the sun breaks through a smog-filled Calcutta winter morning. I visited the tribal village of Darra Adam Khel where the children of Kalashnikov dealers arm themselves with cricket bats to play on their school grounds; the war-zones of Sri Lanka where, between bullets and bombs, the game of cricket goes on in spite of, or perhaps because of the civil war; in the most unlikely surroundings, such as the searing deserts of Rajasthan, watched only by a camel and its owner, a farmer plays on the sand with passing travellers. Cricket is played by what appeared to be everyone. And it is certainly played everywhere.

The game is not restricted to those who play. Cricket mania is so widespread, so deeply etched in the psyche, that it has the ability to touch on the lives of people in a variety of ways. The passion filters into dusty one-room workshops in Sialkot and Meerut, where the sun streaming through the windows reveals craftsmen laboriously hand-stitching cricket balls; the old scorer at the prestigious Calcutta Cricket and Football Club who has not missed a single Sunday match in fifty years; carpenters who leave their native Gujurat every season and live on the streets of Jaipur to turn out cheap cricket bats; inside the oldest scoreboard in Sri Lanka, a mass of ladders, wooden platforms and iron wheels operated by boys who lurk in the shadows.

It is these characters—the unsung heroes and not the famous cricketers on the international circuit—that tell the real story of the game on the subcontinent. They will never appear in newspapers and their games are even less likely to appear on television. This idea drove me to investigate the people who carry the game to its ultimate glory; the back-street players who instinctively carry out the rituals via a natural instinct—a passion found in every generation for nearly 200 years.

I did not photograph the Imran Khans, Kapil Devs or Aravinda De Silvas. Instead, I recorded the enthusiasts who, in their imagination, are playing in a World Cup Final in front of a screaming crowd of 100,000 fans at Calcutta's heaving Eden Gardens. Here, the reality of the alleyways in Old Delhi, where cardboard boxes become makeshift stumps and a line of sandals mark the bowling crease, is easily forgotten.

To try to explain the reason for my quest and the purpose of my pilgrimage is not easy. It is perhaps best described as a journey of discovery into the very essence of subcontinent cricket and into the area's grass-root culture. Perhaps like any religious pilgrimage, I was searching for answers. But it was definitely an alternative cricket tour.

FIELDS OF DREAMS

In the vast grassy expanse in the midst of Churchgate, a dozen men were sitting cross-legged on the grass. They were huddled in a circle, playing cards and gambling with tatty rupee notes. Next to them, a cluster of boys with a dilapidated bat, one pad and one ball between them, shouted with fury as their fielder missed an easy run-out opportunity. Fifty feet away an inter-office match was already half-way through its forty overs, fielding two more conventional-looking teams in immaculate whites, with umpires and an official scorer. The malis, the unofficial groundsmen, were dragging a roller over the adjacent pitch. Nearby, a vendor was selling bottles of luminous liquids in various breathtaking hues from a large barrow, to the hundreds of thirsty young sportsmen. The whole area was a checkerboard filled with games of cricket that often looked a little too close for comfort. In the background, the majestic buildings of the Victoria Terminus and St Xavier's College formed an impressive backdrop to Bombay's financial hub. This was a typical Sunday afternoon in Azad Maidan and encapsulated the very essence of maidan cricket.

Not just there for the cricket—the maidan also plays host to other forms of entertainment. Azad Maidan, Bombay.

Maidans exist in almost every city, town and village in the subcontinent. Literally meaning "open space", the Indian maidan is often likened to an English park. Whereas a park is usually a place to seek refuge from the noisy crowds to relax in an oasis of calm, the chaos and noise of an Indian city extends to the maidans.

Although a widespread activity throughout the subcontinent nowhere is maidan cricket more evident than in Bombay. It has the ability to capture not only the sporting atmosphere and importance of the game itself, but also provides an arena for the understanding of a more widespread culture and lifestyle which cannot be witnessed elsewhere. Bombay is fondly known as "the nursery of Asian cricket"—where the maidan takes centre-stage.

A bird's-eye view (from the top of the Bengal Cricket Club pavilion) of Shevaji Park, Bombay. A breeding ground for young stars and home to many of the great Indian players of today.

This arena can be compared to a theatre, a circus of activity: it is a cabaret of high drama, the interaction of the audience strongly resembling that of a pantomime; each actor contributing his own personality and character to the production. As I spent that Sunday afternoon threading my way through Azad, Cross and Oval Maidans (all adjacent to each other) it was difficult to know where to look first, such was the frenzy of activity. I saw a sporting arena that was a galaxy removed from Headingley in my native Yorkshire. There the atmosphere is usually as cold and damp as a typical English spring morning.

Cricket, as my first lesson in the subject went, is not only a national obsession and identity; culturally it is far more meaningful, creating the framework for the entertainment to take place. It has the ability to unite

The daily net practices continue every afternoon in Metunga Maidan, Dadar in Bombay (where Sunil Gavaskar began his playing days).

a nation and to represent the qualities and characteristics of urban India. Nowhere more than the maidans of Bombay is such a cross-section of urban society better represented; displaying a diversity of wealth, profession, ability, caste and age. The beauty of maidan cricket is seeing all these elements combined in one glorious encounter.

Although the whole city is effectively one gigantic cricket ground, there are particular concentrated areas of activity. The middle-class suburb and Maharastrian stronghold of Dadar is one such place, home to Shevaji Park—a breeding ground for young stars. Shevaji Gymkhana, the original club of the late Vijay Manjrekar, one of India's all-time great batsmen, stands here, one of the many clubs on the circumference of the maidan. It is also the coaching ground of Ramakand Achrekar. A modest, unassuming man in his sixties, who has devoted his time to coaching young stars, the most recent of which being Sachin Tendulkar and Vinod Kambli.

A couple of miles away is Metunga Maidan, home to four cricket clubs including Dadar Union. It was here that Sunil Gavaskar began his playing days—continuing to play for the club even during his international career. The maidan now looks grubby and neglected. The tin shacks that act as pavilions and club houses are battered and long past their former glory. The malis who tend to the ground and pitches, live in tents on the circumference of the maidan which is overlooked by concrete apartment blocks. It may appear undignified, especially when compared to the manicured lawns of the Cricket Club of India or Bombay Gymkhana Club. Yet no institution in India is nurtured with so much love and attention. Like the Hindu lotus flower emerging from a murky pond, the beauty and grandeur of Indian cricket blooms from the rough and shabby earthiness of the Metunga Maidan.

For the enthusiast and spectator alike, Marine Drive, sandwiched between the Arabian Sea and railway lines along the sweep of Back Bay is an unforgettable sight in the long shadows of a late Sunday afternoon. It is here that a string of Gymkhanas were formed during the 19th Century by the richest members of various communities. It was once said that if ever India was to achieve communal harmony, it would first take place on the cricket field. This string of grounds, on which the Parsee and Hindu Gymkhanas are situated, is evidence of that common thread which binds religions together through cricket.

The malis take out a heavy roller to prepare the pitch for the next match. Wilson College ground on Marine Drive, Bombay.

These clubs still thrive and the hundreds of players who use the grounds demonstrate not only tolerance and co-ordination, but display a distinct lack of fear under such dangerous conditions. The danger? It is one thing to be aware of a cricket ball, since everyone acknowledges the impact of cork on flesh at high speed and protective guards shield them accordingly. However, when 12 matches are carrying on side-by-side, a fielder is more likely to be hit by a ball from another game than his own. A slip fielder, whilst attentively watching the batsman and the direction of the ball flying off the bat, has as much chance of being whacked by a well-struck six, lofted over deep mid-wicket from a match taking place on the other side of the maidan.

Cricket is not just limited to weekends. Every weekday at 7 am, practice nets are dotted over Azad, Cross and Oval Maidans. Before work, office workers cast aside their shirts, ties and briefcases and exchange them for cricket whites. As the steady stream of commuters pours along the footpath from Churchgate station, the players lose themselves in practice for two glorious hours before work. At 9 am they pack up their kitbags with extreme reluctance, the nets come down and another working day begins.

It was one evening at Azad Maidan, in front of the prestigious Bombay Gymkhana Club, that I met Pankaj. He was a diminutive boy only marginally taller than his bat, with his pads reaching uncomfortably to his thigh. This was not surprising since Pankaj was only five years old. He was going through his daily batting practice with his father: standing in the nets at a little over three feet tall, his face was a picture of intense concentration as he faced every ball that his father bowled to him. A left-hander of immense diligence, the consistency of Pankaj's forward defensive strokes would have made Geoff Boycott gape with wonder. A small crowd of interested onlookers gathered as they were passing on their way to the station after work. One of them remarked to me with pride, "We call him our Lara of Bombay." No doubt if young Pankaj carries on with the same degree of assiduity in his future years, he will certainly be breaking records at some stage in the 21st century.

But the "cradle of cricket" offers far more than mere Sunday afternoon entertainment to "cricketing tourists" like myself. The maidans of Bombay hold a remarkable power over the nation's sporting customs and achievements. It is not only the immense popularity and mass appeal that makes cricket so meaningful but also the way in which the game is so efficiently organised in so many tournaments. The Ranji Trophy—the domestic inter-state tournament—which has been won by Bombay 30 times in the past 58 years. There are more than 70 local tournaments a year; from the Times Shield, an inter-office tournament in which 311 teams compete, to the rather soggy Kanga League which brings together 98 teams who play in the monsoon season. With over

Young players' practice match during the daily coaching session, at Dadar Union's ground (Sunil Gavaskar's old club) in Metunga Maidan, Dadar, Bombay.

A concrete slab is a familiar sight, a common surface for the wicket in many of Karachi's maidans.

(opposite) *After the day's play: the pavilion/dressing room/clubhouse at Azad Maidan, Bombay.*

The Panther and Tiger's Club and the Ludhiana Gymkhana are two of the many clubs that practice side-by-side at the MAO College grounds in Lahore.

At five years of age Pankaj already shows signs of being a star batsman. His father coaches him at Azad Maidan, Bombay, everyday after school.

The grounds of the Central College in Jaffna holds most of the this war-torn city's cricket matches and coaching. In the background is the old library bombed some years before.

10,000 registered players in the city and over 50 turf wickets, Bombay is the largest cricket "workshop" in the world: a factory geared to nurturing and developing India's favourite game.

There can be no starker contrast to the playing conditions in Bombay than Karachi. Far from the luxurious expanse of nurtured grassy maidans, Karachi's cricketers are handicapped by the lack of open space and amenities. And what space is available is rough and barren. On a tour around Karachi's urban areas of Nazimabad, Korangi, Orangi and Liaqadabad, the conditions were so poor that it is a credit to the local coaches and players themselves, given such conditions, that Karachi has produced so many of Pakistan's great players.

It was not uncommon to see a playing surface consisting of just a concrete strip in the midst of a treacherously uneven and stony ground. One maidan I visited in an urban estate, can only be described as a wasteland: from the road, I had to walk through a boundary made up of a rubbish dump and nearly tripped over the rotting flesh of a donkey, long dead, lying in the middle of household waste. Something unidentifiable was smouldering in one corner, sending black smoke curling towards the sky in the direction of large birds circling vulture-like overhead. A few feet away, a boundary fielder was oblivious to his environment as he concentrated on the next ball, a rather fast delivery to a tail-end batsman. The ball flew in his direction and he could have prevented a boundary by flinging himself to his right along the ground, an act which any Bombay outfielder would instinctively have done. But not surprisingly, with risk of injury by scraping himself across the ground, he was forced to concede the runs.

Not every Karachi maidan had such a difficult playing area, but considering it is a stronghold of Pakistani cricket, it astonished me that so many great players were able to develop their cricketing talent in a city so obviously lacking in facilities. The climate, hot and dry for most of the year, means that there are few areas of grass, in the city, which only added to the problem. Karachi is one city where the emphasis of grass-roots cricket is definitely found on the streets.

TEA
8
14

(above) *The "Funny Guys", a team from the local Jain community in a district of Bombay, appear in the final of a "Triangles" tournament together with the Black Panther Club. Far from displaying the ferocious characteristics their name suggests, the 1995 Polo Cup, was played in a typical maidan atmosphere but with the organisational skills that made the whole afternoon proceed like clockwork.*

(left) *Sheltering under a canvas awning, at a club match at Azad Maidan, Bombay.*

(above) *The ninth wicket goes down in a club match at the Oval Maidan, Bombay.*

(opposite) *A bright Sunday afternoon at Azad Maidan, Bombay, with the grand colonial buildings providing a stunning backdrop to the cricketing activities.*

(top) *Hyderabad is a major stronghold of Indian cricket, bo 6000 matches in 13 divisions, and is the home town of Mohe med Azharuddin. In the Parade Ground, one of the maidar where Azharuddin started his playing days, this inter-bank tournament brought together Central and Syndicate Banks. ground is not the official home of any cricket club, which invariably means that there are never any permanent facili for the cricketers, not even a pavilion. However, a more temp rary, though rather obscure shelter, was made available in t police buses. They were parked in a line at the edge of the m so that the back of the spacious vehicles could be used as a*

combination of pavilion, dressing room, shelter from the sun and as a venue for team strategy meetings.

(opposite middle) *In Shevaji Park, weekdays in the late afternoon see the arrival of people returning from school or work. Seven year old Ajit, using his school bag as a wicket, is coached by his father everyday. His father, who used to play cricket at club level, is anxious to see his son succeed.*

(opposite bottom) *From the celebrations at Sharjah, to the more informal but equally joyous activities at Azad Maidan, cricketing victories are always accompanied with music and dancing. There were trophies, cash prize money, an official presentation and even a band which played with gusto to accompany the closing stages of the 20-overs final. Dinesh, Lokesh and the rest of the "Funny Guys" (the winning team) dance to the beat of the tabla, watched by a decent-sized crowd seated on folding wooden chairs, and the relatively sedate guests of honour.*

(above) *On a cold and frosty morning in Delhi a well-wrapped bunch of players use a motorcycle helmet in an imaginative way to form part of their cricket equipment.*

In Shevaji Park, rude interruptions are often caused by wandering wildlife or on this occasion a herd of cows. It is then the responsibility of the outfielder to shoo them away.

Coaching for women is all too rare in most countries, and especially in the subcontinent. But in Shevaji Park, Bombay young women are coached every week. It is here that most of India's national women's team begin their playing days.

An apartment block looms over the Dadar Union, in Metunga Maidan, where Sunil Gavaskar used to play. Dadar, Bombay.

The workers' clothes are hung up and forgotten about, as every afternoon they leave the drudgery of office life behind them. At Shevaji Park, Dadar, the ground fills up before and after work every day.

In Calcutta's Esplanade a flock of sheep disturb the batting practice of college students during their lunch break.

In the background stands the imposing Eden Gardens, the most hallowed turf in India. Undaunted by its intimidating presence, more down to earth maidan cricket goes on.

Calcutta is home to one of the world's most significant sporting venues: Eden Gardens. With a capacity of 120,000 it usually fills its stands during major matches. Opposite this immense stadium is the Esplanade, or the Calcutta Maidan, host to a different form

of Calcutta's rich cricketing culture. A vast green expanse in the heart of the city's smoky, smoggy, industrial sprawl, the maidan becomes an oasis of tranquility dotted with informal cricket matches being played at all times of the day. In front of that other colonial reminder, the Victoria Memorial, the students taking an extended lunch-break between lectures to play a game. The area is usually more crowded at weekends, when competition for space, like every major maidan, is intense.

The winter sun rises slowly in the misty Calcutta sky as the malis drag out a heavy roller in preparation for the coaching sessions at Desha Priya Park.

In Madras, the Triplicane area has always had a strong cricketing tradition. Close to the seafront, the Marina Ground is one of best-known club grounds in the city. Here an outfielder tries desperately to outstare a buffalo enthraled by the game.

Five-year old Pankaj, the latest cricketing prodigy from Bombay, hard at work during his daily batting practice in the nets.

Iqbal Park, probably the Azad Maidan of Lahore, where net practice is a common activity throughout the day.

In sharp contrast to Bombay's vast grassy maidans, facilities in Karachi are meagre, often wasteland with a concrete wicket and treacherous outfields. The players on this maidan have to compete for space with a herd of goats.

Multan in Pakistan is also home to cricket enthusiasts. And nowhere was devotion and commitment more aptly demonstrated than by nine-year old Wajid, whose right leg was deformed at birth. Having to walk with crutches did not restrict nor discourage him from playing cricket. Wedging a crutch under his arm he adroitly balanced himself for the shot. Persistence and doggedness made this young player stand head and shoulders above any other I saw.

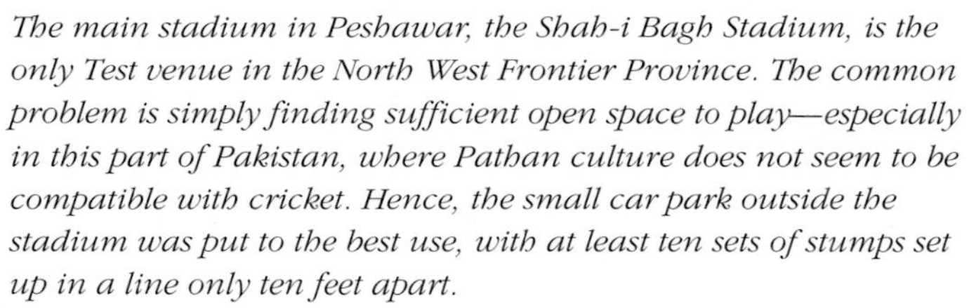

The main stadium in Peshawar, the Shah-i Bagh Stadium, is the only Test venue in the North West Frontier Province. The common problem is simply finding sufficient open space to play—especially in this part of Pakistan, where Pathan culture does not seem to be compatible with cricket. Hence, the small car park outside the stadium was put to the best use, with at least ten sets of stumps set up in a line only ten feet apart.

It often seems as if the entire population of Lahore is out playing on Friday afternoons, so much so that one becomes accustomed to seeing every available scrap of grass, street and park being used as a playing venue. Yet to discover that the dangerous surface of the railway shunting area of Mughulpura was the home of a semi-official ground was something of a revelation. In between the railway tracks that criss-cross the dry earth the games carry on the players seemingly oblivious to their surroundings.

The old polo ground in Karachi is now a regular venue for cricket; a pile of bricks substituting for stumps is a common sight.

(opposite) *Twin towers of Pakistani culture: in the background is the Minar-e Pakistan built in 1960 to commemorate Pakistan's independence. In the foreground, the mark of a more long-standing culture, the ubiquitous bricks signify where the match will start. Iqbal Park, Lahore.*

DAWN

A barefoot bowler practices in Iqbal park, Lahore, with the Minar-e Pakistan in the background.

A peep inside the Liaqat-bagh in Pindi reveals a match between schoolboys before they return home in the evening.

Afghan boys, true to form, seem to have a fascination for graveyards, here in a rural districts of the NWFP.

The grounds where such players as Waqar Younis and Wasim Akram started playing and where they still practice, is also frequented by the neighbourhood lads. Practice grounds behind MAO College, Lahore.

Iqbal Park, Lahore. Whilst most players are satisfied to play on a surface of worn grass or concrete, others have higher standards. One team literally "install" their own pitch for every match they play. This portable surface is made up of scraps of canvas, roughly sewn together and stuck with tape, then pegged to the ground. And it is easily transportable: rolled up like a carpet it can be balanced on the back of a bicycle and taken home to be stored ready for the next game.

HOTEL
AKBAR
INTERNATIONAL

One of the fairer sex is given a rare opportunity to play with her brother, in Pindi's Liaqat-Bagh.

Substitute stumps come in all shapes and sizes—an abandoned bicycle is "borrowed" for the purpose.

(opposite) *The long shadows at dusk in Pindi, Liaqat-Bagh, one of the many parks in the country which are taken over in the afternoons for cricket.*

INTO THE MADDING CROWD

Cricket crowds have to be seen to be believed in the subcontinent. Before experiencing a cricket match there, I could never have imagined the atmosphere, passion and excitement that accompanies the game. A far cry indeed from the matches I used to attend at my local grounds in Yorkshire; in England people watch a cricket match. In the subcontinent, they celebrate.

Whether in the heaving stands of Eden Gardens for a Test Match with a crowd of 100,000, or a local club match, it is the manner in which the spectators wholeheartedly throw themselves into the spirit of the game. There is always a vibrant display of partying and participation, where flags, banners and musical instruments are essential props to create a carnival atmosphere.

Nowhere is such a celebration more obvious than at schools' matches in Sri Lanka. In particular, the Royal Thomian Big Match, the annual encounter between Royal and St Thomas' colleges, which provides the country with not just a sporting occasion, but also a carnival, a reunion—and a three-day party.

Schools' cricket has a special place in Sri Lankan sporting culture and remains the best organised and by far the best-attended level of the game, surprisingly more so than Test Matches with crowds of between 15 and 20,000. Dozens of colleges and schools participate in regular tournaments, and at the end of the season, the major rival colleges meet in an annual "encounter"—a two or three day match which is as much a historical event as a cricket match.

The Royal Thomian, also known as the Battle of the Blues because of their school colours, is the most important event on Sri Lanka's sporting calendar. Aside from drawing the biggest crowds, it can claim to be the second longest uninterrupted school's series in the world, after the clash between Prince Alfred's College, once attended by the Chappell brothers, and St Peter's of Adelaide, which began in 1878, only two years before the first Royal Thomian. The Eton-Harrow match which started earlier was temporarily suspended during World War II.

So what makes the Battle of the Blues so special? From talking to old boys, former and current players, plus reading numerous programmes from previous matches, one word does sum up the occasion: tradition. Coming as I do from a country where the old school tie is now considered largely old hat, it was somewhat surprising to discover that the root of this Sri Lankan tradition seemed more British than the British themselves; complete loyalty to one's old school. An extract from the editorial of the St Thomas' match brochure confirms this: "The only way we can justify the fact that we attend two of the most premier

Pushed against the fence and shouting until hoarse, the crowd thrust hands, pens and scraps of paper in the hope of getting the attention of a passing player. The Bengali crowd are renowned for being the most emotional, vociferous and volatile in India, and have been known to make or break a hero. Many players from around the world claim that there is no greater atmosphere than Eden Gardens, and the feeling a player gets when stepping out into the packed stadium is unforgettable.

However, at a match between England A and India A, the crowd was sparse—made all the more conspicuous in this vast venue. What few people there were had gathered in one corner of the stands to add atmosphere and noise to the event. If any player, from either side, came past them the spectators would try desperately to get their attention to sign an autograph.

(opposite) *At the Brabourne Stadium, Bombay, the Master's Cup brings together international players aged over 35, and provides vintage cricket for a delighted crowd.*

educational institutions in this country is by living up to those traditions and thus, to show the world the best traditions in which this game should be played."

From numerous conversations I overheard in cricket-club bars late into the night, Sri Lankans retain a very proud and strong allegiance to their old colleges—30, 40 or even 50 years after leaving. Old boys return year after year to relive memories, to renew old friendships, and to recall past playing days. Former pupils come to watch their sons, grandsons and nephews following in their fathers' footsteps making the whole event a family affair. While the country's cricketers of tomorrow are battling it out on the field, the past, present and future mingle in one huge and glorious celebration.

Ex-Prime Minister and President, well-behaved in the Mustangs' tent at the Royal Thomian match in Colombo.

Frequent pitch invasions were positively encouraged; a half-century, boundary or the fall of a wicket was greeted by firecrackers and smoke bombs along with animated shrieks of approval. People of all ages danced to a bizarre fusion of rock, eastern rhythms, calypso and jazz that poured forth from the performing bands. In the true style of Sri Lankan hospitality, I was welcomed into the throng with enthusiasm. The fact that a cricket photographer who loved to dance happened to be a woman caused much interest, astonishment and amusement. Reluctantly, I had to refuse the constant offers of alcohol persistently waved in my face, explaining that focusing a camera whilst inebriated is a little tricky.

The allegiance of each supporter is proudly displayed with the respective colours of their college (blue and black for St Thomas, blue and yellow for Royal). Hundreds of flags fluttered in the breeze, and the stewards from each college ensured their respective pupils gave their team audible and fervent support. Headscarves, T-shirts and wristbands made from woven cotton were on sale in the street outside the ground, and supporters drove around the streets of Colombo with their college flags flying outside the windows to drum up as much enthusiasm and attention as possible. The event invariably captures the imagination of the whole city—even the newspapers devote most of the sports pages to coverage of the match.

Fun and frolics is a popular source of entertainment at any Indian game. A Ranji Trophy match in Bombay between Bombay and Baroda at the RSC ground in Bombay.

However, back in the early days of the "Big Match" there was never the same degree of celebration that one finds today. An extract from one centenary brochure recalls the early years when, "No flags were waved, no lower-school boys shrieking with delight, and lastly no old boys making the queerest antics in appreciation of the play and recalling the old incidents and relating their thrills to their admiring sons, nephews and grandchildren."

Today, however, it was not only the younger element who let their hair down. It was definitely a time for the "older" old boys to re-live their youth with a heady mixture of dancing, drinking and relaying bawdy jokes. The Mustangs have a significant role to play in this. Formed in 1918 by a group of ex-pupils from both colleges who met regularly at matches, they felt that some institution should be organised to maintain their friendship and to encourage the continuation of what had become a great tradition and social event. The first formal meeting in 1920 elected a president, and from then on the group has been the haven of a prestigious élite.

The Mustangs' exclusive tent was full of High-Court judges, high-profile businessmen, government ministers and MPs. But for three days their social status was forgotten as they prided themselves on drinking the most whisky, singing the filthiest songs, teasing any unfortunate woman who walked past (including me), and generally behaving like adolescents again. A strict "no ladies" rule prevented me from entering the hallowed Mustangs Tent and nothing could bend the staunch chauvinistic rules but I was content to hang over the barrier and absorb the infectious party spirit.

I stood enjoying the mood of the event and, to put it mildly, the informal atmosphere of a gathering of people usually seen in more formal situations. "Have you ever seen anything like this before?" slurred the company MD, as he swayed gently in front of me, food stains visible down his silk shirt. I answered that no, such events do not exist anywhere else. He edged closer: "This is a hangover from the British, you know," he whispered confidentially, as he swigged the last drops of malt whisky from his bottle and staggered off to join the group of distinguished lawyers to sing the next round of rugby songs.

Ticketless fans at the Ranji Trophy match between Bombay and Baroda have to be satisfied with sitting outside the ground to watch the play.

Estimable lawyers, politicians and businessmen act anything but respectable as they let their hair down in the prestigious Mustangs' tent at the Royal Thomian match in Colombo, as they dance to rock, eastern rhythms, calypso and jazz.

(above) *Nothing sums up a supporter's allegiance stronger than a flag; whether for their country, local team or school. And nowhere is the presence of flags more conspicuous than at school matches in Sri Lanka, where it is obligatory for all pupils to wave and wear their school colours. Vans and cars full of students race through the streets of Colombo, flying the flag out of the window to drum up attention and support from passers-by.*
(below) *The colours of each college are made by enterprising souls here selling headbands, scarves and wristbands made of woven cotton outside the ground at the St Joseph's and St Peter's Big Match in Colombo.*

In harmony with the more sedate atmosphere of the Battle of the Saints, the Rectors of the two Catholic schools were sitting in the pavilion; dressed in their immaculate white cassocks their calm presence offering their own dignified support. As the match programme stated, cricket is "a game that can foster correct values and healthy attitudes" which explained why none of the more usual antics were tolerated at this match. I asked the Rector from St Joseph's his opinion of the game of cricket, and why it was so significant in instilling the values which the college and The Catholic Church would approve of. "Actually," he confessed, much to my surprise, "I don't really like cricket—I prefer rugby. Cricket is too boring." However, he did feel that cricket offered more virtuous qualities than other games and that good and wholesome lessons that could be learned from the sport.

(above and left) *At the St Joseph's and St Peter's annual Big Match in Colombo.*

Alcohol has a major part to play in the celebrations at the Royal Thomian match in Colombo. The crowd certainly enter into the spirit of things.

In the hallowed calm of the pavilion at the Sinhalese Sports Club, home of Sri Lankan cricket, the St Joseph's College caretaker absorbs himself in the Big Match. Standing majestically, next to the Wall of Fame of past cricketers, he watches with undivided attention, never moving from his post outside the players' dressing room.

Slightly more subdued at the Ananda Nalanda Big Match, two Old Boys sat sedately in the stands, silent throughout. With an ear glued to a radio to catch the commentary on the match, there was no swigging away of liquid refreshments for these supporters who were much too engrossed in the match itself.

(opposite and above) *Sharjah provides a venue which enables India and Pakistan to compete on neutral turf, since neither country will risk hosting a match at home for fear of crowd trouble. The large local population of Pakistanis and Indians turn out in full force, both inside the ground and out.*

Outside Eden Gardens in 1995 the fans waited for over an hour at the end of the match to catch a glimpse of the England A team players. These supporters formed a large crowd on the main road much to the concern of the lathi-armed police, who often seem a little overzealous in their work. The fans clamoured for a precious signature for their autograph books, and with their hands reaching into the bus windows, they possibly overawed many of the players who were not familiar with such exuberance.

THE POWER OF THE SMALL SCREEN

A crowd of half a dozen men sat in a chai shop, sipping out of chipped cups with their eyes glued to the black-and-white television set perched on a tiny shelf. Seemingly oblivious to each other and their surroundings they were mesmerized by the images on the screen. An exciting moment and the tension increased. The owner was momentarily suspended service and time stood still.

The reason for everyone's interest in the television was the live action from the Asia Cup in Sharjah, beamed by satellite into almost every building in the locality. The Asia Cup is just one of several competitions created to allow India and Pakistan to play each other on neutral grounds—to play on home territory would mean transforming the spectator stands into battle zones—and games are followed with feverish patriotism. This year was no exception, especially as Pakistan, the pre-tournament favourites, were being beaten by Sri Lanka.

Whenever an important match is shown on television it usually means good business for chai shops, cigarette stalls and restaurants which are transformed into spectator arenas with the attention focussed on tiny black-and-white monitors. This is especially true during an overseas Test series. During transmission-time work is usually abandoned and normal life grinds to a halt as people congregate around the nearest television set. (A recent sociological study in India calculated that more days are lost to the workplace during a major cricket series than to illness—an indication of the power of television and how much the game is worshipped.)

In Rawalpindi, I followed the progress of a game as I wandered down the high street in the busy commercial area on the Murree Road. From chai shops to chemists to cigarette stalls, even a washing machine shop. As the game progressed and it became more and more obvious that Pakistan were on the verge of losing, the crowds became more and more distraught. I watched the final overs on a television that nestled comfortably between chewing gum, toilet rolls and packets of paan hanging from the top of the kiosk where rickshaw drivers, businessmen, newspaper sellers and policemen blocked the pavement and became increasingly emotional. As the game died and Pakistan's demoralized players trooped off the pitch, the pavement audience dispersed and returned reluctantly to their normal working day.

Gathered around the TV sets in Pindi where the whole country was engrossed in Pakistan's game against Sri Lanka in the Sharjah Cup.

GAMES IN THE GALLIS

Chowri Bazaar is one of the many markets in the maze of streets in Old Delhi, more noted for a babble and tangle of cycle-rickshaws, hawkers, cows and pedestrians mingling with constant noise. Tucked behind in relative peace is Galli Paswan, where on a Sunday afternoon the most likely sounds are a thud, clang, cheering and clapping.

Sunday street cricket in the *gallis* (literally meaning "narrow street") never ceased to amaze me: it was always an entertaining and unique display of imagination and neighbourly tolerance. *Galli* Paswan is little more than eight feet wide, with three-story stone houses on either side. The space is barely adequate for the batsman to attempt much more than a straight drive to the bottom of the alley, which was about 30 feet long. This, of course at least eliminated the necessity for slip, deep mid-wicket or square leg fielders.

As soon as the ball makes contact with the bat, it usually ricochets off each wall several times before being retrieved at the bottom end of the galli. There, fielders at the bowler's end attempt to prevent the ball reaching the wall behind them, which provides the only boundary. Luckily, all the windows on the first two floors were protected by a set of brightly-coloured heavy metal bars, saving a vast amount of rupees on what would have undoubtedly been replacement window panes. The only other fielder was the wicketkeeper, standing guard behind the obligatory wooden crate, competing for space with the umpire and remainder of the batting side who make their presence known by constant cheering and encouragement.

(opposite and above) *Galli Paswan in Old Delhi, the narrow confines of the alley means that the rules of the game have to be adapted.*

When attempting to score, the best tactic for the batsman was to hit the ball towards the roof, in the hope that the ball would hit several washing posts, windowsills and alcoves before bouncing back to the ground, giving him time to scamper a couple of runs. The small band of spectators observing from the rooftops also doubled up as high-altitude fielders, leaping across the rooftops if the ball failed to return to ground level. That was commonly acknowledged to be six runs, although a lost ball meant dismissal for the batsman, as well as a severe reprimand from his fellow players due to the cost of replacing it.

In the bizarrely named Slave Island, a working-class residential area in the centre of Colombo, the streets are transformed every Sunday. It was here that I saw one of the most unusual examples of street cricket. At the end of a side-street, just off the main road, was the batsman. A few feet away was the bowler, who gently lobbed a tennis ball to him. The batsman then skied the ball over the bowler's head, and over to the other side of the road, where three fielders were placed. The passing trucks, buses and cars merely made fielding more unpredictable, as the fielders often lost sight of the ball until it bounced to the ground. The idea was to catch the ball before it bounced, without it hitting a passing vehicle. Extra runs were awarded if the batsmen could lodge the ball onto the roof of one of the opposite shops; a nifty shin up a drainpipe would then enable it to be retrieved.

Street game in Paharganj, New Delhi.

Of all the hundreds of street games I witnessed in the subcontinent, this one, although not taken as seriously as usual, was the most entertaining and amusing. Even if passing cars were hit, no driver would bother to reprimand the players. There seemed to be no point; it was an accepted part of street life and so was not deemed to be "wrong".

Around the corner onto the quieter Glennie Street next to a suburban railway line, I learned of the real role of the wicketkeeper. The stumps, a wooden crate placed in the middle the road was such that any average size car or van could squeeze by on either side. However, on the odd occasion that a bus or truck trundled up the street and was too wide to pass, the wicketkeeper was responsible for moving the crate to allow the driver to pass.

Bombay, being the cradle of Indian cricket, not surprisingly has a well developed system of street cricket. The area of Fort, the centre of the banking area in the centre of the city, contains some of the quietest streets on a Sunday, the only traffic-free day.

At around 7 am, local teams—usually made up from the workplace or neighbourhood—arrive early to stake their claim on a particular street for a couple of hours. Somehow the system worked so that everyone had a chance to play on their particular "turf", even though competition for space was fierce. Often the roads used are the main streets crossing Churchgate, and here, the wicketkeeper looked on nervously as a red double-decker bus, another throwback to colonialism, inched its way around the stumps.

Another major cultural phenomenon in Pakistan is the movie industry. Larger than life cinema billboards depict evil ogres, voluptuous scantily-clad heroines and swarthy moustachioed heroes who come alive on every street. Songs from films are perpetually blasted out of crackling radios in every tea shop, taxi and corner store. Anyone who experiences that travelling nightmare, the video bus, has to endure back-to-back Hindi or Urdu films throughout the night. The songs are played full blast through the worst quality speakers imaginable, thus the familiar tunes remain engraved, reluctantly, on the memory.

Thankfully, no such agony is suffered in the name of cricket. In Lahore's old city, the two cultures fuse together in blissful harmony as the relatively quiet streets openly invite players from the locality.

(opposite) *In the middle of the commercial area of Bombay, Fort, the streets empty on a Sunday and the area is taken over by endless ribbons of street games. Here, the boys are setting up their stumps—just a plank of wood—ready to start their game.*

लॅन्ड
डिजनी

In the heart of Triplicane in Madras, the Sunday afternoon traffic usually has to avoid several matches being played in the middle of the roads.

The traffic-free streets in Bombay's financial district on a Sunday provide ideal playing surfaces.

Clean bowled in a street game in Dadar, Bombay.

On the streets of Dadar, rules are adapted so that boundaries are realistically set.

Street game in Paharganj, New Delhi with a rare girl-player.

In the business district of Fort in Bombay.

All in the business district of Fort in Bombay.

Avoiding the midday sun, young cricketers commandeer Slave Island in Colombo every Sunday morning and evening. Java Road is especially popular. The most bizarre: skying the ball across the main road where the fielders have to try to prevent it from going over the roofs of the shops on the opposite side of the road.

In Slave Island, Colombo, it is also the wicketkeeper's job to move the box being used as a wicket to allow a vehicle to pass.

Java Road in Slave Island, Colombo, in the long shadows of a late Sunday afternoon.

Lahore, Friday afternoon, improvisation is the name of the game.

Old Anarkali, one of the oldest parts of Lahore, is often the venue for impromptu games.

An old man chats to a magazine vendor while trimming his moustache: cricket and movie magazines are given equal billing, two of the main leisure activities in Pakistan.

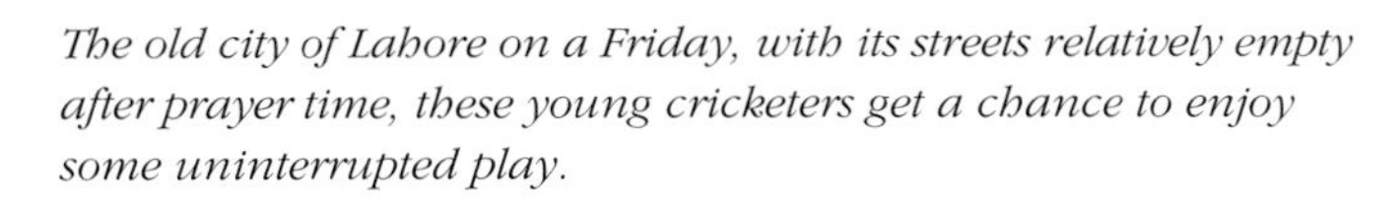
The old city of Lahore on a Friday, with its streets relatively empty after prayer time, these young cricketers get a chance to enjoy some uninterrupted play.

The main road leading out of Lahore's old city, on a usual traffic-free Friday.

Old Anarkali in Lahore's old city, just behind the main road.

The cinema hoardings loom larger than life in this Lahore backstreet creating a colourful backdrop.

LEATHER & WILLOW

An axe in his right hand, Ratan Singh eyed me carefully as I stopped my bike on the roadside. Four of his grandchildren ran up to me, tugged at my clothes and thrust 12-inch cricket bats in my face. With small bats selling for Rs.5 (10p), with a full size bat priced at Rs.20 (40p) and a set of stumps at Rs.15 (30p), three families have established a business and somehow scrape a living making and selling equipment at these prices. These carpenters leave their native state of Gujurat to come and live and work on the streets of Jaipur in Rajasthan for six months every year during the cricket season.

They live in a tatty row of canvas tents behind their working area, the pavement littered with mounds of adu, a cheap local wood. The men, women and older children worked methodically to transform the rough and uncut wood into a mountain of bats and stumps of every conceivable size to suit customers of every age. Surrounded by piles of wood shavings, they first hacked away at the pieces with small axes, and gradually the wood was whittled and planed into more refined shapes. The black rubber handles were made from old car tyres, demonstrating a widespread Indian practice, mainly through economic necessity rather than environmental awareness, of recycling everything.

An optional extra were stands for stumps. These are specially designed, and are essential for street cricket, where it is simply not possible to push or hammer stumps into the surface of the road. Also available were miniature bats about a foot long specifically designed for autograph collecting. This, second only to playing seemed to be the other main pastime for cricket lovers everywhere in South Asia.

The finished products lined the kerb attracting passers-by. The younger members of the families had obviously been taught the more aggressive sales techniques; any potential customer who showed the slightest interest in any of the goods usually went away with more than they intended. I certainly did.

In the heart of the old city of Hyderabad, surrounded by teeming bazaars and choked by diesel fumes spewing from the passing traffic, is the Charminar monument. It was built in 1591 by Mohammad Quli Qutab Shah to commemorate the end of a plague, and is one of India's best known examples of Islamic architecture. The monument is one of Hyderabad's most recognizable landmarks and is even immortalised on the cigarette packets of the same name.

Almost as eye catching a feature is sight of the women who shade themselves from the burning midday sun under buses or umbrellas; selling bats and stumps to local boys, lining them up on what little space was on the roadside. Every so often, a small team of boys wheel

In a dark, dusty workshop in Sialkot, a craftsman puts the finishing touches to a pair of cricket pads.

(opposite) *Hand-stitching the tough leather of a cricket ball, in a small workshop inside the old city of Sialkot, Punjab, Pakistan.*

Piles of rough uncut wood are quickly transformed into bats of all sizes, many of which will be sold overseas. Workshop in Sialkot.

up their rusty bicycles and ponder over the equipment on show. With all the earnestness and expertise of diamond experts, they picked up each bat in turn, carefully contemplating its quality, weight—and probably cost. After a brief consultation they handed over a few crumpled rupee notes, their purchase was complete. Strapping the goods to the back of their bikes, they weaved their way back into the traffic and back to their local maidan, to show off their new prized possession.

The manufacturing of sports equipment is big business in South Asia and the cities of Meerut, near Delhi, and Sialkot in Pakistan are both internationally famous. Football, hockey, boxing and of course cricket equipment is produced in factories of all sizes, ranging from small backyard cottage workshops to massive factories run by world-renowned companies such as S G Sports and Grey Nicholls who export thousands of bats, balls, pads and gloves to be sold throughout the world under some of the best known brand names.

When one watches a humble cricket ball being hurled down the pitch by a bowler or being hit for a six it is difficult to appreciate the amount of time and labour that went into producing it. Whether in a small one-room workshop or a massive factory the sights and sounds are essentially the same, as are the production processes. There are no modern automated production lines, just good old-fashioned craftsmanship. The only difference being that in the smaller factories a single craftsman handles the complete production from beginning to end,

whereas in the larger factories a team works together with each individual stage finished by a different man. To make a cricket ball a few strips of cork are first hammered into a rough spherical shape, this is then tightly bound cotton thread like a ball of wool until an even sphere of the correct shape has been formed. Two pieces of red leather are then sewn together using an invisible stitching process and moulded into two perfect hemispheres. The cotton-wrapped cork is then encased in the two hemispheres of leather to be stitched again, this time with the double-row raised stitches to produce the famous seam so vital to bowlers. The ball is then ready for the final stages of heating, varnishing and polishing before being packed into boxes by the dozen like so many rosy red apples ready to be shipped overseas.

One factory owner proudly told me that an Australian company experimented in manufacturing cricket balls by machine, but failed in their attempts to match the high quality of the handmade product.

The industry is important to the economies of Meerut and Sialkot where it seems as though almost every family is involved in making sports equipment. Whether it is cutting yards and yards of canvas for batting gloves or pads, or transforming piles of uncut Kashmiri willow into bats of all sizes with the higher quality products destined to be exported and the lower quality being retained for the domestic market. Sport has provided employment and international acclaim—all because of a bat and a ball.

(above) *Pieces of cork are bound tightly with cotton thread to produce the inside of a cricket ball.* (left) *Leather is moulded into hemispheres to be sewn together. Workshop in Sialkot.*

The final stages to the ball: after moulding, hammering, stitching and dying, the ball is then varnished and heated. Factory in Meerut.

Ratan Singh puts the final touches to a stump made from Adu wood on the pavement in Jaipur where he lives.

Old city of Sialkot, Punjab: (top) *In the streams of sunlight the tailor cuts sheets of canvas to make batting gloves, in his workshop in the old city of Sialkot, in Punjab.* (above) *Using a heavy-duty manually-operated sewing machine a craftsman puts the final touches to some batting pads.*

(left) *A true cottage industry: Meerut also contains hundreds of family-run workshops, producing bats, balls and stumps in exactly the same process as the large factories.*

(top) *Bats for Sale: outside the Charminar Monument in Hyderabad. In the midst of the teeming bazaars, the maidan cricketers haggle with the vendors.* (left) *A conveniently parked bus gives some relief from the midday sun.*

(opposite) *Inside one of the largest factories in Meerut, this carpenter, part of the production line, prepares a bat for its final varnish.*

run for murder brought his skills to the area. Almost every shop in this Wild West town's bazaar is a dimly-lit workshop where craftsmen make or copy any gun imaginable, from Smith & Wessons and carbines, to guns disguised as pens or walking sticks. An experienced gunsmith can produce the exact replica of almost any gun in ten days. The shop-owners lounge around on charpois waiting for customers. Men come to the town from all over the country to buy weapons, either as a status symbol or in the case of tribal people as part of their traditional way of life. The eerie silence was often shattered as cutomers fired off a round of bullets in the direction of the distant hill to test the guns before they made a purchase.

Whilst applying for my permit to visit Darra at the Civil Secretariat's office in Peshawar the senior official recognised me from a previous visit three years earlier when I had stayed with a family of gun-dealers. This meant that work in the tiny office was brought to a happy end for the day as all the staff decided to celebrate the fond reunion by drinking karwah, a local green tea.

The following day I took a cramped bus for the 30-mile journey over the sandstone hills in the Kohat Frontier Region to Darra. As I stepped off the bus, out of nowhere a stocky, bearded Pathan joined me. He was dressed in a dark grey uniform and carried the ubiquitous rifle over his shoulder, his beaming smile revealing his betel-stained teeth. After he repeated several jumbled phrases, it dawned on me that he had been "assigned" as my personal guide. He asked me for my permit and then proceeded to give me a guided tour of the bazaar. As I did not have the slightest interest in buying a gun this was definitely what I didn't need. The chances of obtaining any information from him on cricket seemed rather remote and eventually he took me to a friends shop who fortunately spoke reasonable English. After drinking several cups of tea I discovered that there was an inter-village tournament starting that afternoon in the mountains. Whilst anticipating the event with relish, my guide reappeared ready to cart me off to another shop. However, on learning of my intention to visit the cricket match he glared at me and made it perfectly clear in no uncertain terms that I was upsetting his own plans for the rest of the day.

"No, no! Government paper say you leave by one o'clock. Only two hours here. Kidnapped." With this dramatic declaration, it did not look as though it would be easy to budge him. It was obvious that a third opinion was required as neither of us seemed prepared to concede. We ended up going to another shop where another pot of karwah was produced to smooth the nogotiations. I desparately tried to explain to the shopkeeper (another gun-dealer and occasional journalist) that the only reason for my presence in Darra was to photograph cricket, and official permission had been authorized. "Let me stay until 2 pm," I moaned. But my guide was adamant that I should not be let loose in the wild expanse of the mountain villages—cricket or no cricket. "No. Government say fighting. On the news."

I turned to the "journalist" for salvation. He was obviously in a dilemma. Although he had an obligation as a Pathan to assist any visiter, we was undoubtedly under instructions to help to get this "stupid foreigner" out of town as soon as possible. He informed me that fighting had broken out in the mountains and kidnapping was a real possibility. More tea arrived and the gun-shop owners brother arrived to announce that unfortunately the weather, it seemed, had clouded over unforgivingly and therefore the tournament had been cancelled. As I looked at the clear blue sky I found this weather report somewhat dubious. Nevertheless, I had no choice in the circumstances but to reluctantly abandon any plans to see what surely would have been a very unusual cricket game.

The sons of gun-makers play outside their school in Darra Adam Khel, in the heart of the tribal area of Pakistan, where the sound of gun-shots often echo around the distant hills.

Everyone looked relieved. The Guard, for getting his own way, was now beaming again and tried to drag me once again around the gun-shops. Eventually, I made a deal with him. If he took me to a couple of local schools to enquire about cricket, I would get on the bus back to Peshawar, as requested. We slithered across the road—the only street in Darra which was thick with mud caused by the constant stream of heavy lorries passing through. We walked across a muddy field to a junior school; a one-roomed wooden hut where 50 boys sat on the floor reading in unison from a book. As soon as I walked in, all the children, who were about ten years old, stood up and recited something to me. They then sat down again this time politely facing me. After explaining to the teachers what I was looking for, they beakoned me to the window. I peered outside. In front of a breathtaking backdrop of sandstone coloured mountains a group of boys wearing their uniforms of black shalwar kameez and Chitrali hats had just started to put up their stumps. I even smiled at my guard who was already bored with the whole affair.

The remaining boys trooped outside followed by their teachers who had to abandon any thoughts of continuing the lesson. I loaded a film into my camera watched by a 100 pairs of solemn black eyes. It was clear that the reason for my visit remained an eternal mystery to them, although by this stage of the trip I was accustomed to the baffled looks I received. A young batsman cracked a ball in the direction of the road and, as if answering an echo, a sharp retort of gunfire came back. I did wonder whether any of the boys would abandon their traditional way of life to pursue a more unconventional career—like playing cricket.

Desert village, Sam: It did not seem possible: in the searing heat of the deserts of Rajastan, on sand-dunes that stretched as far as the eye can see, somebody, somewhere was playing cricket.

Calcutta is home to one of the world's most celebrated sports arenas: Eden Gardens, with a maximum capacity of 120,000. Opposite this vast stadium is the Esplanade, or Calcutta Maidan, which has played such an important part in the social and sporting history of the city and is a breeding ground for cricketers. A vast green expanse right in the heart of the city's smoky, smoggy industrial sprawl, it is an oasis of tranquil lity in one of India's most densely populated cities. Taking full advantage of this green lung the maidan is blanketed at any time of the day with cricket matches. Students and office workers alike take every opportunity to set up their stumps for a game before or after work, during lunch-breaks or even between lectures.

The maidan also faces the Victoria Memorial which was built as a monument to Victoria, the Empress Queen. It was conceived by Lord Curzon as a rival to the Taj Mahal in Agra, and like the latter was built of white marble from Rajasthan and, as a feature of Victorian town planning, was surrounded by a beautiful garden. Parks and gardens, as with the Esplanade, are one of the great legacies of the Victorian colonial period throughout its former colonial possessions.

In the Punjabi village of Hassanabadal, a few miles outside Islamabad a batsman carefully watched as a bolwler began his run-up. He stepped two paces down the wicket and with a deft flick of his wrists he turned the ball to the boundary. It hit the wicker mesh of a charpoi for a well deserved four runs. As I approached the players, the entire village population emerged from a large house next to the playing area, all dressed in their best clothes with the women garlanded with flowers.

The charpois, it materialised, were "borrowed" by the players from the hosts of a wedding as their boundary. There were sufficient charpois to surround the entire playing area which prevented the ball from disappearing into the river or onto the main road at opposite ends of the ground. All the village members were attending the wedding between a 34-year old carpenter and his bride, everyone had lent their charpois to the wedding household. Amongst the solemn wedding ceremonies local boys made use of the charpois in a way probably not aniticipated by the host.

It did not seem possible. In the searing heat of the deserts of Rajasthan, on sand dunes that stretch as far as the eye can see, somebody somewhere was playing cricket.

When I discovered that in the village of Sam children play for their local camels and their keepers it was too irresitable to miss. As the jeep drove us from the old fort city of Jaiselmeer we gradually left civilisation behind and arrived in a barren landscape of never-ending sand. As if a mirage was appearing out of the sand, was the unthinkable, the surreal, the unexpected.

A lone camel stood solidy, looking characteristically bad-tempered. A farmer from the village was testing his skills against a group of boys from Calcutta who probably had never seen the desert sands before. It was therefore only fitting that they should experience the delight, if not unusual playing surface and conditions, of the fine white powdery sand on the gentle rolling sand-dunes.

Varanasi, situated on the banks of the sacred Ganges, is the holiest city in the world for Hindus. It has been a centre of learning and philosophy for over 25 centuries ever since Buddha preached his first sermon in nearby Sarnath, one of the most beautiful sites in the world. To die at Varanasi or to immerse the ashes of a loved one in the Ganges is believed to ensure liberation from the cycle of mundane life and the attainment of eternal life. It is, quite simply, a great place to die.

Varanasi is also a major tourist attraction and the best way to view the city is to take a boat-ride downstream, preferably at dawn when the morning casts its warm rays on the temples and the river is crowded with bathers during their daily worship. It is a classical image found in every guidebook.

On the afternoon I was there I met Madan Lal who runs a chai-stall with his brothers at the east end of the Dasaswamedh Ghat. He disappeared for ten minutes only to return with a bat and a bright red rubber ball and began setting up a wicket along the flat slopes of the ghat. Playing cricket along the ghat was precarious, especially for the "outfielders"; a firm shot could send a ball towards the river where flowers, rotting wood and other rubbish floated by. Madan Lal and his brothers were able to manage their chai-stall by rushing back everytime a customer approached the stall, otherwise the game carried on watched by boatmen, street-sweepers and priests in ochre robes.

(top) *Varanasi, Ghats: Situated on the banks of the sacred Ganges, the "Eternal City" one of the most significant pilgrimage sites in India.* (Above) *Bhubaneswar, the capital of Orissa, is renowned for its many temples.*

Ghandi Beach, Madras, the children of fishermen gather to play every Sunday.

Outside the Qasim Bagh Mosque, Multan.

Galle Face, Colombo

(right and below right) *The seafront on the Galle Face in Colombo is often as crowded as any beach resort in the world.*

In front of the Parliament Building, in Battaramulla, Colombo.

Multan, the largest town in southern Punjab, and the centre of Pakistan's main cotton-growing area is also noted for its many shrines and mosques dating from the 13th and 14th Centuries. Opposite the Qasim Bagh Stadium, where international matches are held, three half-bricks substitute for a wicket in an impromptu game, with the stunning white mosque inside the Qasim Bagh fort in the background.

The Shah-i Bagh Stadium in Peshawar is the only Test playing ground in the North West Frontier Province. Like most cities in Pakistan Peshawar suffers from a lack of open space for cricket. Here the small car park opposite the stadium has been commandeered by at least eight sets of stumps set up in a line, with only about ten feet between them. Such is the pressure for even this space that two shifts operate on the usual busy Fridays.

Sri Lankan cricket: Paddy fields at Miriswatta; Coconut plantation in Indigolla; The Dutch Fort in Galle; a bowling crease at Galle Face, Colombo.

On the beach at Mahabalipuram in south India, more famous for the shore Temples in the background.

Railway tracks just outside Lahore.

(opposite top) *A game at the east end of Dasaswamedh Ghat at Varanasi.*

(opposite bottom) *The old town of Lingaraj, in Bhubaneswar, more famous (in guidebooks) for its Hindu temples.*

(above) *Ashok Puram, a district in Mysore, is part of the largest settlement in India of the Harijen, the lowest caste, orginally the untouchables.*

(right) *One of the many temples in Bhubaneswar, the capital of Orissa.*

The Red Fort, in the heart of Old Delhi, is one of the most famous examples of Moghul architecture in the country. It is also one of the only open spaces in the area available for cricket.

Even washing lines can be used to denote a boundary as in this maidan in Delhi.

A cold and frosty winter morning in a park in New Delhi, using a motobike helmet for stumps.

The end of a day's play, in a small ground next to the Ferosha Kotla International Ground in Delhi.

The buffalo moving across the pitch only hold up play for a few moments, in the villlage of Shadara, near Lahore.

(left) *The Fort in Lahore is a major tourist attraction in the city, but does not hold enough interest for everyone.* (opposite) *The old city of Lahore is a popular venue on Fridays, especially the gardens outside the Badshahi Mosque.*

Afghan children in a village just outside Peshawar.

In the village of Ambar in the North West Frontier Province workers in the cement factory take a lunch break.

A club match with two local teams at a maidan in Nazimabad, a district of Karachi.

Afghan children playing in the village of Shahmansoor, in the Swabi district of the North West Frontier Province.

THE CAREER OF A LIFETIME

Somewhere in the suburbs of Calcutta, the sun struggles through a bleak winter sky on a Sunday morning at dawn. Barely illuminated in the ghostly yellow light, with its background formed by the grey silhouettes of the concrete building behind, stands the breeding ground for the next generation of budding stars.

Wiping the sleep from their eyes at an hour when most sane people are still tucked up in bed, boys stagger along to Desha Priya Park for their coaching sessions weighed down with kit-bags and equipment and trickle slowly into the pavillion. Stretching, running and twisting figures in the chilly air signal the start of the exercise session while the malis drag out the heavy rollers to prepare the pitch.

For four days a week, this is a typical start to the day. The nets are already up and batting practice is underway, whilst a young wicket-keeper leaps off the ground for an overhead catch.

Desha Priya Park is one of about 150 coaching centres in Calcutta. More significantly though, they see cricket as a passion transformed into a career. The direction and perception of the sport in India has radically altered over the past decade; with so much at stake and with so much to gain, cricket is now seen as a gateway to anything from a full-time job to stardom.

Major companies have been involved in sponsoring cricket in India since the mid-1960s. After the major banks were nationalised in 1971, the State Bank of India continued its involvement, mainly by taking cricketers onto its payroll. However, in the mid-1970s the bank decided that sportsmen should no longer receive special favours and job applications had to go through the normal channels. Other companies from new industries swiftly stepped in to fill this vacuum as they found cricket provided an ideal medium through which to promote their products and to improve their corporate image through public relations.

For this reason success as a club cricketer in India, Pakistan and Sri Lanka can offer enormous financial rewards and fringe benefits as well as the security of a job from a bank, airline or other major industry. And, as two cricketers who played for a bank and a local district in Peshawar told me in a chai shop cricket presented one of the few opportunites for overseas travel, being financially beyond the reach of the average person in Pakistan.

Even more enticing nowadays is the prospect of lucrative contracts from advertising and endorsements. Often on a par with movie stars in terms of status and hero-worship, top players are used to advertise everything from soft drinks to clothing. In any tea-shop down one of Bombay's many backstreets, the poster on a darkened grubby wall will

Players at the Ananda Nalanda match waiting to bat, in the comfort of the pavilion at Khettarama Stadium (top). *In contrast to the Afghan boys at a very rough ground in Mera village of Akora Khattak* (bottom).

One boy starts off young. (top) *Emphasis is placed on technique and repetitive practice.* (above) *Both at the Sports Coaching Foundation in Chacha Nehru Park, Hyderabad.*

often feature the beaming faces of Sachin Tendulkar or Vinod Kambli drinking a local brand of fizzy drink. Likewise Wasim Akram is likely to be seen in nearly every advertising break on Pakistani television promoting a similar well-known soft drink.

The best players of the modern game can vastly increase their earnings through sponsorship deals with manufacturers of sports equipment, appearance money in benefit matches as well as playing English county cricket. Cricket is a money-spinner and players take full advantage of the fees they can demand.

The massive increase in financial support for the sport from sponsors, and their willingness to invest far more into the game is mainly as a result of the massive boom in media coverage which has in part been fuelled by the growing number of cable and satellite television channels. With cricket having such a large following it is not surprising that more and more tournaments are being devised specifically it seems to fill the available air-time. A good example was the seniors' tournament held in Bombay in 1994 which featured older cricketers from eight Test-playing nations with many well past their prime and long since retired from the modern competitive game. All the players had to be over 50 years old, but such is the reverence for cricketers—past and present—that this tournament commanded huge audiences Asia wide on satellite and also allowed them to enjoy the limelight once again.

With the prospect of a full-time job, a decent income, international travel, private endorsement contracts, as well as the glory of being a star, it is not surprising that cricket has become such a competitive business. More and more youngsters are attracted to the game, which has been instrumental in the increase in coaching facilities, and there is enormous competition to be accepted as a pupil. There was a time when boys were only under pressure to succeed in their general school education. Nowadays one is just as likely to see middle-class parents investing their money in their sons' cricket coaching, on the understanding that success at cricket can be a stepping-stone towards getting a rewarding job. It is certainly an incentive that attracts thousands of boys into the practice nets every day before school.

Cricket coaching has entered into a new era. The early 1990s have seen an increase in coaching facilities and well-equipped academies are being opened. One such example is the Sports Coaching Foundation in Hyderabad. Only founded in 1994, it has answered the need for more high-tech facilities: it contains the only bowling machine in India—a device imported from America originally designed for baseball batting practice and can hurl the ball at a maximum speed of 185 kph. It also has floodlights, duel-coloured sightscreens and astroturf. Twelve coaches, six of whom are Ranji players, supervise each session whilst sports psychologists and nutritional experts ensure that each child receives an all-round education about health and fitness. A game-planning board, a scaled-down model of a playing field, using wooden models and plastic chips to help youngsters develop an appreciation of the game. Serious training, and far more than just broken nets in a goat-field...

Sai Baba, the brains behind the academy, has invested time, money and total commitment in setting up his brainchild. Its purpose is to train boys and girls between the ages of 6 and 16 in the fundamentals of the game. Emphasis is placed not only on learning the technicalities and skills but also to teaching a correct approach which ensures an understanding of the game in all its aspects. Such an approach commands a more professional attitude. A serious foundation built in a professional manner, taking the game—and the money it commands—very seriously.

The coach at the Vappalani Sports and Recreation Club in Madras, whilst not having quite such an impressive array of equipment at his disposal, still displays the same dedicated commitment as his more youthful counterparts. Well into his 60s, he has been coaching every weekend for the past 30 years. The club only pays his petrol money on his motorbike to and from the club. His sole reward is the deep satisfaction he gains from coaching which he does solely from a love of the sport. "God has given me enough money to live on," he explained, "and now I am retired I can repay the pleasure I got from cricket by teaching youngsters".

His was a common approach—one which understood that the principles and values instilled in boys through playing cricket will stand them in good stead in everyday life. In his informed opinion "the qualities that cricket encourages include those such as discipline, respect for elders, teamwork and dignity". Proving that cricket is not just a sport—it is also an attitude of mind.

Hanif Mohammed, who until he was overtaken by Brian Lara, held the world record for the highest first-class innings. He still plays a major part in Pakistan's cricket development and coaching at the Defence Stadium in Clifton. (above) *The bowling machine at the Sports coaching Foundation, Hyderabad.*

M.C.H. SPORTS COACHING FOUNDATIONs
HYDERABAD INDUSTRIES LIMITED

It is generally unusual for any emphasis to be given to coaching girls, unlike these local orphaned girls who are given free coaching at the MCH Sports Coaching Foundation in Hyderabad. (opposite middle) *Matting wickets are something of a rarity in Rajasthan; this is one of two at the Jaipur Club. The club was originally a social club but now has a wide choice of sporting facilities.* (opposite bottom) *Two Ranji Trophy players practice their under floodlights at the Sports Foundation in Hyderabad.* (above) *A dawn practice session on a cold winter's morning at the Desha Priya Park.*

WILSON COLLEGE GYMKHANA

A SENSE OF HISTORY

Murree

Muree sits on a ridge amongst pine forests in the cool bracing air of the mountains in the North West Frontier Province and serves as an oasis from the burning summer heat of the cities.

The foothills of the Himalaya have served as a summer retreat for centuries, but it was the British who adopted them for their own. Enterprising officials of the Raj built dozens of hill settlements with quaint bungalows, majestic hotels and churches in the early years of the 19th century, often taking a perverse delight in weather that was "just as wet, windy and wretched as England". Countless balls, dinners, sporting events and picnics created a resort atmosphere that contrasted sharply with the surrounding forests. Today the hill stations are as popular as ever, still British in origin, now transformed into a thoroughly South Asian institution.

It must be surely one of the most spectacular backdrops for any cricket ground: situated at the top end of the village the ground commands a sweeping panoramic view of the surrounding hills. It belongs to the Army Public School (established in 1990) and during my enquiries to find out if any matches were due to be played it wasn't long before I found myself sitting in front of the stern headmaster. Wishing I did not have so much mud on my scruffy shoes as I felt like a naughty schoolgirl in front of her headmaster. As luck would have it a game between two college houses was scheduled for that afternoon.

Although storm clouds were rolling in menancingly over the village the rain held back until the evening and I was treated to an unforgettable afternoon's cricket, which I watched sipping tea out of white china cups and eating biscuits. It seemed rather appropriate that given the British influence on both cricket and the village of Murree, I should find myself enjoying the game in such style.

The scoreboard at the Karachi Gymkhana which records the historic win by Pakistan over the MCC in 1952.

Karachi Gymkhana

There can be no greater contrast to the rough maidans of Karachi than the prestigious Karachi Gymkhana, the oldest club in the country. It was the venue for Pakistan's historic win over the MCC in 1952, which enabled Pakistan to become members of the International Cricket Council; thereby gaining Test status. The scoreboard from the match is proudly displayed on the pavilion wall, recording that memorable event.

Although no test match has been played there since the 1970s the club still attracts the weathier members of Karachi's society. Offering a host of other sports facilities besides cricket. The club runs three cricket

(opposite) *The Wilson College Pavilion along Marine Drive in Bombay.*

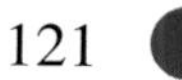

The storm clouds roll in over the Army Public School ground in the picturesque hill-station town of Muree, Pakistan.

teams: the regular team which plays in several local tournaments, a veterans team which plays every Thursday, plus a junior team. Even though there is a joining fee of Rs 20,000 a long waiting list still exists to join the club. Rather than the noise that usually accompanies games in most parks and maidans, the only distraction here, apart from polite rounds of applause, is the ringing of members mobile telephones.

Mohammedan Sporting Club

Not grand, not elegant, and certainly not a picturesque setting. The exterior of the Mohammeden Sporting Club opposite the mighty Eden Gardens in Calcutta can only be desribed as shabby and dilapidated.

Sports and recreation has always played an important part of social life in Calcutta. One aspect of this was represented by the social clubs set up by the elite society of Calcutta at the time of the Raj. The original clubs set up by the British were exclusively for whites; some of them even sported notices stating that dogs and natives were not allowed entry. Replicating the lifestyle of the British elite, anglicized Bengalis set up similar clubs of their own. The Mohammeden Sporting Club being one such club that was originally a Muslim cricket club.

Sports form an important part of the social history of the subcontinent and a sporting spirit naturally became identified with nationalism. When Mohan Bagan, the premier Bengali club of Calcutta, defeated a white team to win the Indian Football Assosiation Shield in 1911 it was an occasion for the entire city to rejoice. But the sporting field also became a scene of Anglo-Bengali camaraderie. Thus Bengal's first win in the Ranji Trophy, was a combined effort of both English and Bengali players.

Journey to the Highest Ground

"Welcome to the Switzerland of the East" proclaimed the blue sign as I stepped off the bus. It was 4 pm and it had taken me nearly twelve hours from Delhi by various modes of transport to reach Chail, the tiny hill station holding claim to the highest cricket ground in the world.

Unfortunately I had failed to bear in mind that during February at 2,500 metres in the Himalaya, the climate would be rather chilly compared to the deserts of Rajasthan where I had spent the previous two days. However, determined to reach the shrine, that hallowed turf, I ventured on up the steep incline of the hill, desparately attempting to reach my destination before frostbite set in. My shoes, not ideally suited for the conditions, marched me into a driving blizzard and were soaked within four paces.

With my camerabag firmly on my back and completely enveloped in an enormous blanket, I bore a striking resemblence to a cross between a Yeti and the Hunchback of Notre Dame. I must have presented a rather dramatic sight to the rather more enviably and sensibly dressed Sikh, safe inside his thick overcoat, warm wollen socks, and snow boots all topped off with a gently glowing pink turban. "How far to the cricket ground" I asked between chattering teeth. He looked at me very apologetically and said: "actually the cricket season hasn't started yet as the weather is too cold". I tried to explain that rather than to see an actual game, I was there purely to see the ground, which had been a long-standing ambition of mine. Whether he understood the rationale behind my mission was not clear, but he seemed happy enough to accompany me up the hill.

After a couple of kilometres we eventually reached our destination, and the huge sense of achievement made me forget all my physical discomfort. The only clue to suggest I was standing in front of a cricket ground (after all, snow covered grounds must all look pretty much alike) was a tiny forlorn pavilion and two large slabs of stone marking the wicket. I think Mr Singh, a physical education teacher was rather impressed with the speed at which I had reached the top of the hill. He pointed out the official notice, as proof and to satisfy me. "World's Highest Cricket Ground, Height 2,444.4 metres. Designed in 1893 under the direction of His Highness Bhupinder Singh, Maharaja of Patiala."

At the "Lovers' Quarrel", the Big Match between Mahinda and Richmond colleges at Galle, southern Sri Lanka

The maharaja, as well as giving so much entertainment and notoriety to the game, was also the captain of the first All-India team to tour England in 1911. There was a close friendship between the rulers of Patiala and the great Ranji Singh, and it was Maharaja Bupinder Singh who donated the gold Ranji Trophy. To promote the game in India, the maharaja was responsible for bringing over such greats as Rhodes, Hirst, Larwood and Tarrant and also sponsored the first Australian team to tour India, in 1935.

His highness is one of the delightfully eccentric characters that make up the folklore of cricket history in India. This larger-than-life character enjoyed an equally large appreciation for cricket and women—he had several hundred wives and concubines in his palace. On one occasion, when playing for the MCC and sporting one of his garish turbans, a game was held up for several minutes when he lost one of his large pearl earrings.

I had the impression the Mr Singh thought I was just as eccentric. After we bade our farewells, I saw his turban shaking from side to side rather incredulously as he trudged back down the hill.

At the Azqar Ali Shah Stadium in Nazimabad, Karachi. An amusing name has been given to the heavy roller.

As the sun set and I slithered down the hill, I decided that treating myself to a night in the old Palace, now a hotel, had to be the ideal way of ending my pilgrimage. Willing to spend some extra money on a touch of decadence, I looked forward to the splendour and luxury of dining and residing in a royal household. Well, for one night anyway, as I had to return to Delhi early the next morning.

Unfortunately, my illusion was very soon shattered a few minutes after I had checked into my room. A power cut meant there was no light, heating or hot water. After complaining to the reception staff—and refusing to accept "it will be back on in five minutes, madam" they realised that it would be far less trouble (and would probably keep me quiet) if they built an enormous log fire in the bar. I sank deep into the leather armchair a few feet away from the fire and consoled myself with a large brandy.

The electricity never came back on during the night. The heat from the roaring fire—and the internal heat from the brandy—grudgingly made me grateful for the slight increase in my body temperature. Other than that my journey ended as it had begun. Cold.

Galle Cricket Ground

Whilst some grounds are famous for their history, others are noted for the atmosphere. Without doubt the most breathtaking setting of any ground I visited was the Galle Cricket Club in southern Sri Lanka.

I arrived in Galle by bus from Colombo. It wasn't difficult to locate the ground as it was immediately adjacent to the bus station. I hestitated at first, as I surveyed the ground through strands of barbed wire. I soon realised my hesitancy was uncalled for because what I saw was imposing and emcompassed every element, both man-made and from mother nature, to create the most idyllic setting.

From the press box situated on the second floor of the old wooden clubhouse the view was spectacular, with the deep blue ocean on the right, narrow streets and old stone houses on the left with the magnificent old Dutch fort in front. The spectators sat on the ramparts swinging their legs lazily over the sides.

The "Lover's Quarrel", as the Galle Big Match is enticingly called, was so named because Galle has such a close-knit community and most students and their families enjoy close ties with their counterparts from other schools. The intense rivalry that exists in the Big Match games in Colombo does not extend to Galle.

The shabby exterior of the Mohammedan Sporting Club in Calcutta.

(above) *The world's highest ground at Chail.* (opposite) *A colonial atmosphere remains at the Lahore Gymkhana, the oldest cricket club in Lahore.*

RCF-SUPHALA
RCF-SUPHALA
सुफला

HATTON NATIONAL BANK

BIG BOYS PLAY AT NIGHT

In the darkened depths of a tailors shop in a Calcutta backstreet there was a poster on a wall, taken during the 1992 World Cup. It pictured Imran Khan, the captain of the winning team in his bright green Pakistan strip holding up the trophy. Underneath, the caption read "Big Boys Play at Night".

Ever since Australian tycoon Kerry Packer introduced his floodlit limited-overs cricket, the sport has grown in popularity and competition is far more intense than in test matches. It attracts larger and more fanactical crowds and can now reach a much wider audience since the spread of satellite television. With the game compressed into a single day it has enabled international tournaments to be organized on a regular basis. With players wearing brightly coloured "pyjamas"—tracksuits in assorted hues of blue, green and yellow—floodlit cricket can enjoy greater visual impact on televised games. A far cry from the sedate atmosphere of white-clad test matches, scorn the purists. Whatever the criticism, there can be no doubt that with its blazing lights and dramatically faster scoring rates this form of the game is fast-becoming the most popular permanent feature on the international cricket circuit.

In many major cities in India and Pakistan where the game has been adapted to suit the local conditions, there is not the sort of razzmatazz found in international games, nevertheless these tournaments create just as much local excitment. Tournaments are held throughout the year, especially during Ramadan (or Ramzan) in Pakistan and in Muslim communities in India when games will start at midnight after the daily fasting and continue through the cool hours of the night until 4 am. The tournaments are either held in small grounds under floodlights or on deserted streets under normal street lighting.

In Bombay's northern suburb of Dehisar, I was invited to the annual Anand Nagar night underarm box-cricket tournament. This was organised by the Om Shiv Sai Sports Club, in a middle-class residential area of the city in the midst of grey concrete apartment blocks. The playing area resembled a tennis court in size, shape and surface. It was played under lights that were specially rigged, Heath Robinson style, for the tournament and miles of electric cables hung dangerously throughout the spectators' area. It was a perfect example of how the game could be adapted to suit the local conditions.

The rules were very simple: each match was six overs per innings, with teams of eight players. The pitch was surrounded by a three-foot high wooden fence over which a red cloth had been draped. They played with a tennis ball which was covered with chalk so that the umpire could see exactly where the ball bounced to avoid any heated

OM SHIV SAI SPORTS CLUB
ANAND NAGAR YOUTH CLUB
NIGHT UNDERARM BOX
CRICKET TOURNAMENT 1995
"ANAND NAGAR"

disputes. This particular measure proved vital whenever the ball may or may not have hit the red cloth. A ball hit straight into the boundary without touching the ground was counted as six runs, four if it touched the ground before hitting the cloth. If the batsman hit the ball straight over the boundary fence he was automatically out. In addition the batsmen had to run between the wickets as normal for a single.

The chances of being bowled were minimal with a soft tennis ball being lobbed underarm, and fielding seemed to be the crux of the game. The fielders were all crouched like slip fielders ready to pounce on the ball to throw it back for an attempted run-out. What was refreshing was the fiercely competitive nature in which the game was played and razor-sharp reflexes were required in this bizarre interpretation of the game. The organisation was excellent and the tournament was well supported financially by various local community businesses who donated money and paid to advertise on the hoardings that surrounded the commentary box and the outside of the ground. This, along with the entrance fee of Rs 300 from each team all went towards the prize money which was split at Rs 3,333, 2,222 and 1,111 for the first, second and third places respectively.

On the last night before the final, the guests of honour (a local police inspector, a senior coach from the area, a shop-owner who I suspect had donated most of the prize money, and myself as a last minute addition), were all introduced to the players. The pre-match ceremonies were a pot-pourri of all the usual Indian formalities; the official "match cake" was cut as hellium-filled balloons were let off accompanied by a massive cheer from the crowd. A group of young girls in traditional costumes danced (an Indian version of cheer-leaders), which was eventually followed by the obligatory speeches. Indicating that even at this level cricket is taken very seriously.

The final itself was between the United Cricket Club and Varjhar and was watched by a large crowd made up mostly of men and boys. For the surrounding housing blocks this also provided a welcome form of free entertainment, mainly for women and girls who I could see silhouetted against the lights in their flats. The commentary box was well lit and the outside of it was decorated with garishly painted advertisements. Inside was a silk covered table on which the winner's trophy stood. A team of three commentators gave a running commentary on the game in loud excitable shrieks.

At midnight, while I had to catch a train, the final was still very much in full swing which was a good excuse for the younger members of the crowd to stay up. As I climbed into an auto-rickshaw to get to the

The "commentary box" (opposite) *at the final of a box-cricket, underarm, tennis-ball night tournament* (above) *in Dehisar, Bombay.*

station, I reflected on one of the most original and memorable tournaments I have ever witnessed.

As I continued my travels, it became evident that this type of competition is a regular occurrence all over the subcontinent and are held throughout the year. In many cities, though mainly in Karachi and Lahore, tatty hand-written posters advertised "tape-ball cricket tournaments". In order for the bowler to gain maximum swing, pace and bounce the tennis ball had to be wrapped in tape, the pitch becoming littered with more and more bits of sticky tape as the game progressed.

Whilst visiting Lahore, I was lucky enough to be invited to attend the Lahore Challenge Cup, a tournament in which an astonishing 264 teams were competing. The event was made all the more remarkable by being held at four different grounds simultaneously, the first tennis-ball tournament at which this had been attempted. It was also the largest competition of its kind ever to have been held in Pakistan.

It was organised by the Shebab-e-Mili, literary meaning "Youth of the Nation", a religious group which had been formed six months previously. A member of the organising committee told me about how much importance they placed on encouraging young people to become involved in sport. This, he explained was the main reason for the event. I asked why they chose cricket instead of hockey or squash, the other two major sports in Pakistan. With slight scorn, he looked at me and said "because everyone likes cricket"—obvious, really.

The competition required meticulous organising. It was sponsored by the *Daily Pakistan,* an Urdu-language newspaper. Again the prize money was made up of donations from local sponsors plus the entrance fees. I went along to the Doongi ground in the suburb of Samnabad at the beginning of the event. It did not take the crowd long to realise that there was a foreigner in their midst and that I was attracting quite a large entourage of amused spectators, and seemed to be generating more interest than the match. A spectator apologised for the "rudeness and inquisitiveness" of the others, and explained "they are behaving like this because you are an alien here," "An alien?" I enquired. He hurriedly rephrased the statement. What he meant, he said, was that most people in the area had never seen a foreign lady before, and wanted to know what I was doing there. Alien or not, I was attracting as much interest as if I had six green legs and had just stepped of a spaceship.

I was ordered to sit in a huge multicoloured marquee, furnished inside with large padded red chairs. This, I was proudly informed, was specially reserved for VVIP's, and I was given constant protection by a selection of "bodyguards". It was from the comfort of this marquee that I watched the rest of the games. The dress code here was strictly whites, so strict in fact, that one game was held up, much to the crowd's frustration, when an umpire sent a player off to change his slightly off-white trousers.

Instead of the concrete courts I had experienced in Bombay, this, whilst smaller, was more like a normal cricket ground with good quality turf. It was also a more recognisable form of cricket with eleven players on each side and most of the "official" rules were observed. The only real difference, apart from being only six overs a side, was that it was played with a tennis-ball. The bowlers were allowed a full run-up and managed a fair amount of pace. The whole tournament last sixteen days and with a first prize of Rs 25,000 (£750) it comanded good press coverage towards the latter stages.

This was all a far cry from the game I had been brought up to understand in Yorkshire, but shows the way the game has been adapted from its original form to fit into everyday use. It is a little more "user-friendly" in some ways and helps keep it alive as a sport. Although it may be disregarded by traditionalists as being the most bastardized version of the game ever played, nonetheless it is ideally suited to local environments, and is a realistic representation of cricket and one in which the skills displayed would make any captain proud.

SCORERS & SCOREBOARDS

He strokes his thick wiry white beard and arranges the coloured pens in order. The heavy black ledger is placed on a wooden table. He settles back comfortably in his chair, waiting for the match to begin. Then he rings a heavy brass bell which was presented to the Club in 1914. Its sharp peals ring out to signal the umpires' entrance onto the field.

The Calcutta Cricket and Football Club is the world's second oldest cricket club—only the MCC is older—and celebrated its bicentenary in 1993. A little younger than that is Mr Samir Dutt, who has been the scorer there for nearly 50 years and is one of the oldest members of the club. In all those years, he prides himself on never having missed a Sunday match and sits in the same upright wooden chair behind the same table, under the shelter of the pavilion.

Once a game is underway—usually local club matches or inter-office tournaments—all the players keep their respectful distance from him in the hushed atmosphere of the pavilion. Once absorbed in the complexities of the task in hand, he speaks to no one and slowly completes the cryptic markings in the scorebook which only other scorers can decipher. He frowns in concentration behind thick glasses, only moving when he holds up his hand to acknowledge a signal from the umpire, or to lift his white china cup of tea, gently sip it and replace it onto the saucer.

A mother anxiously watches her sons at the Calcutta Cricket Coaching Centre.

In Nazimabad, the official scorer had to rely on less gracious facilities. Far from having a table, there was nowhere for him even to sit. He had to be content with leaning against one of the ornately-painted trucks that are a common sight on Pakistan's highways. Using the back of a college excercise book, with only one coloured pen, his work was not carried out with quite the same level of concentration as his counterpart at the CCFC. However, given the unusually difficult conditions, I was impressed.

Scoring is one aspect of cricket that remains a complete mystery to me, and I have the greatest respect for anyone who can co-ordinate the dots and dashes—like breaking a secret code—and record the information in the correct way, as well as calculating the score. Awesome powers of concentration are called for, and it is not an easy task in the heat of the midday sun whether it is leaning against a brightly painted truck at Nazimabad or at Cross Maidan without a pavilion for shade.

Even for the smallest street game in Lahore's Old City, or in gallis in Old Delhi, selecting the umpires and scorer is as important as picking the right team. Times were somewhat tricky when one inexperienced scorer at a match in Colombo got in such a tangle with his columns that he completely lost track of which column was which. It was a con-

(opposite) *Cyril Periera* (centre), *who has been commentating at the St Joseph's v St Peter's Big Match in Colombo for the last 50 years.*

Scorer at the MLA ground, Hyderabad (where Mohammed Azharuddin used to play).

fusing situation: the bowler had bowled a no-ball, the batsman had run a single and one was also run out, but only after they had crossed. Complicated indeed; and unfortunately by the time he had held a discussion with half-a-dozen spectators (none of whom actually seemed to

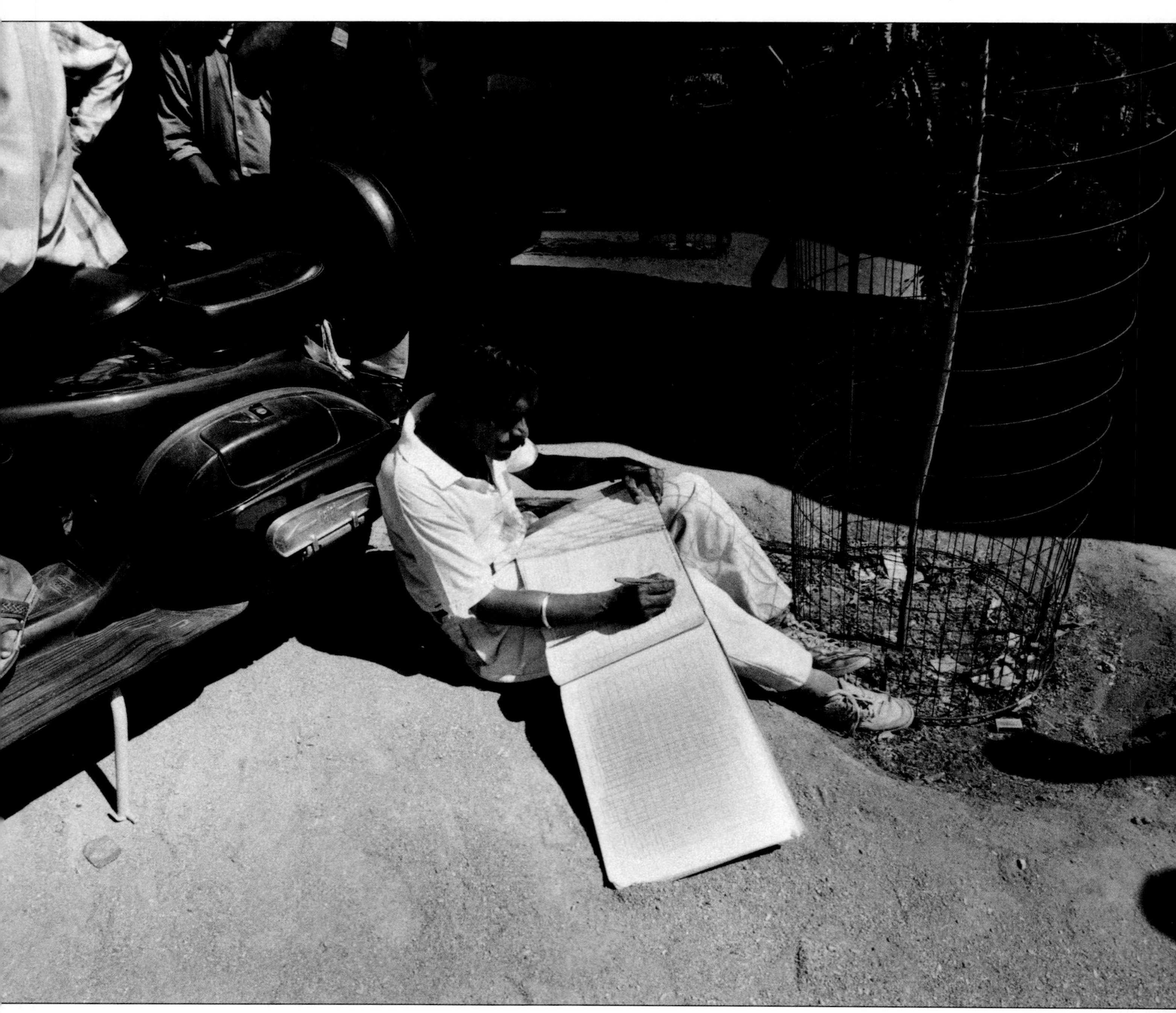

know anything about scoring, but were all quite willing to argue) he had missed another two overs without recording the score. Even after the umpire was consulted—who was 70 years old and had bad eyesight—no solution was offered and the game was brought to an abrupt halt as an argument took over.

Whereas every cricket game had a scorer, it was an indication of a club's superiority if it also had a scoreboard—usually only at more permanent grounds. In many cases it may only have been a rectangular piece of wood, but all seemed to have their own personality; a character which somehow reflected the nature of the venue.

At the P Sara Stadium in Colombo, also known as the Oval Stadium, I was soaking up the atmosphere of the "Big Match" and walking around the boundary, when I came across the scoreboard. Far from being a conventional scoreboard, the exterior resembled a huge wooden box, completely covered with a thick matted coating of lush green ivy. It seemed that I had discovered the oldest scoreboard in Sri Lanka, which was built before World War II.

The interior, after wandering around the back and being summoned to climb up the steep stone steps by two boys from inside, was more like an adventure playground. The inside was made up of a multitude of floorboards, wooden planks, old metal wheels, a series of handles on several levels connected by ladders, plus a collection of numbered metal squares scattered haphazardly over the floor.

It was operated by two young boys who lived across the street, and work at the ground on most match days. Sunlight streamed through the gaps in the metal squares where the numbers and letters were displayed, and we competed for space to peep through to watch the game.

The match taking place was the one-day encounter between St Joseph's and St Peter's Colleges, and all the usual noise and partying was underway in the stands. Inside the scoreboard all was quiet and calm, until there was any action on the field. This caused the boys to leap out from the shadows, turn the heavy iron wheels, shift around the plates with the batsman's name and scamper barefoot up the ladders to operate the handles.

The scorers also sat inside the scoreboard where it was surprisingly well-lit. A natural breeze from the ground supplying plenty of cool air, much appreciated in the intense afternoon heat. No fan or electric light was necessary which was extremely fortunate since the cascade of cables hanging from a dislodged socket on the wall did not look the safest of electrical fittings.

The Karachi Gymkhana, oldest cricket club in Pakistan, where the scorers certainly enjoy more comfort than some of their counterparts in street games.

An inter-office friendly game at the Bihar Cricket Association in Jamshedpur.

BIHAR CRICKET ASSOCIATION
TOTAL
3
1
2
3
9
WKTS
5
BOWLER
1
BOWLER
TOTAL
OVERS
6
LAST
EX-
TOTAL

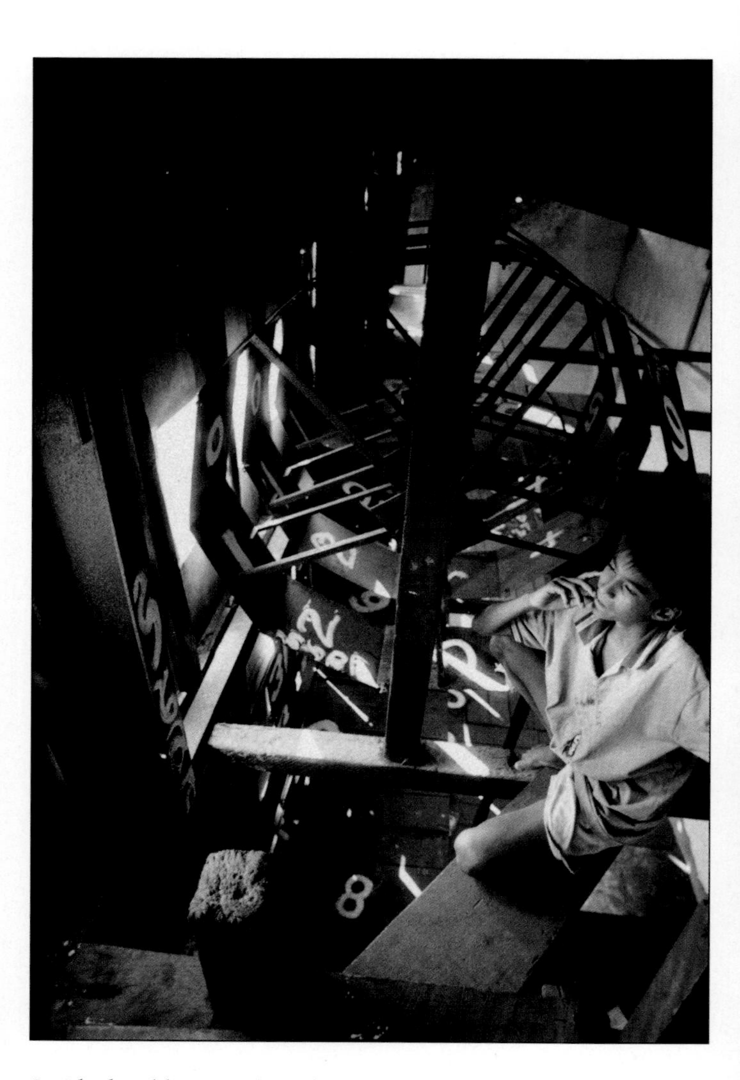

Inside the oldest scoreboard in Sri Lanka, at the P Sara Stadium, Colombo (also known as the Oval Ground) during the St Joseph's v St Peter's Big Match.

SCORER

Scoreboard from an earlier international match, at the Ferosbah Kotla Ground, Delhi.

The scoreboard at the P Sara Stadium with its thick growth of lush green ivy.

BEDFORD
BEDFORD

Mr Samir Dutt, the scorer at the Calcutta Cricket and Football Club, who has not missed a match for nearly 50 years.

The scorer at a street game in Nazimabad, Karachi.